Divine Form Drawing

pre-writing activities through vaishnava stories

created by: Aleena Figueroa

I offer this book to A. C. Bhaktivedanta Swami Prabhupada, and to all of my spiritual teachers who have passed down their love for Krishna.

"The chief function of the child-- his business in the world during his first six or seven years of his life-- is to find out all he can, about whatever comes under his notice, by means of his five senses."
Charlotte Mason, Volume 1

By Krishna's mercy, young children are blessed with the natural inclination to do just this! This means that our job as parents and educators (as all parents are in fact educators) can actually be quite simple. We should encourage our children's innate curiosity, provide an atmosphere where they feel safe and loved, model a healthy and balanced lifestyle, and present them with beautiful ideas that are worth pondering. Providing these basic foundations, there should be no reason for a child to grow a distaste for learning. Why, therefore, is it so common to expect a child to sit quietly and perform shallow repetitive tasks that go against their very nature?

"The mind is restless, turbulent, obstinate
and very strong, O Krishna, and to subdue it,
I think, is more difficult than controlling the wind."
Bhagavad-gita 6.34

Our child's mind will quickly wander if they are not fully absorbed in whichever task they are set to; suddenly it feels as if our effort to teach a child becomes a chore, or worse a battle. Instead of trying to subdue our child's mind, what if we purposefully presented our children with playful explorations that target each of their five senses? What if we consider their need for movement? What if we feed their spirit with devotional stories that nurture their curiosity? What if we could engage our children in this way for each and every one of their academic subjects so that they are eager to learn?

My hope is that the contents of this book will immerse your child's mind, body and spirit in the study of the forms that make up our written language and the world around us.

Choosing Activities

In a general sense, children will develop in similar ways as they grow in mind and body, but when looked at individually, it is evident that each child is truly unique in how their development progresses. If a very young toddler has not properly strengthened the muscles in their legs, it would not be possible for them to stand on their own, and surely not fair to expect them to walk! Similarly, if a 5 year old has not yet strengthened the small muscles in their hand, it could be a painful experience if they were forced to write using a pencil. The exact age at which they are ready for any new task will vary for each child, so we should be careful not to push them into a task that may cause distress or pain.

With this in mind, there are many recommendations for exploring each new form, so you may choose what most engages your child. Watch your child in play, and they will tell you what they are developmentally ready for. Notice those activities your child gravitates to on their own, those games your child does not want to quit, those tasks that your child delights in, then decide which of these activities you would like to introduce. The more fun you have exploring each form, the better prepared your child will be to recreate it on paper when that time finally comes!

Tell a Story

Consider the following hypothetical conversation that might take place after you notice your child is postponing or rushing through an important task. Ask yourself, which scenario do you think will have the most lasting impact on a child's character? Which lesson do you think will stay in their mind long term, even if they may not immediately act on the advice given?

Scenario 1

Parent: "When are you going to start on this?"

Child: "It's easy! I can just do it later."

Parent: "You know, you really should not leave things until the last minute. You say it will be easy, but you should start working on this now so you don't end up with a rushed, sloppy mess!"

Scenario 2

Parent: "When are you going to start on this?"

Child: "It's easy! I can just do it later."

Parent: "Okay. Let me know when you are ready. Have I told you the story of the tortoise and the hare? No? Well, one day, a confident hare noticed that a tortoise was travelling in the same direction as him, so he challenged the tortoise to a race. Who do you think won that race?"

Child: "Hares are super fast! The tortoise is too slow to win!"

Parent: "That's right. And as expected, That hare took off with a *whoosh* and left the poor tortoise behind in a cloud of dust. He got so far ahead he couldn't even see his competitor! You know all that hopping took a lot of his energy, so halfway down the road he stopped for a quick snack. I mean, why not? It isn't like the tortoise had any chance of catching up to such a fast runner as he [you stand proudly]. That hungry hare ate too much though and made his belly ache [you hold your belly in pain]. Suddenly, he felt very sleepy and laid down to let his food digest for a few minutes. Before he knew it, he *snoooooored* hard on the side of the road. He didn't even stir when the tortoise passed him by!

He awoke feeling rested and energized, and continued his journey down the road, all the while thinking about how easy this race would surely be. As the end of the road came into view, the hare saw the tortoise trudging along ahead of him. He couldn't believe it! 'How could this have happened!?' he wondered.

He ran faster than ever [you run in place] as his muscles cramped and burned and his breath [you pant heavily] came short, but still the tortoise was just too far ahead! Even though he closed the gap quickly, he watched in dismay as the slow tortoise calmly crossed the finish line first."

There is a reason that so many of our oldest moral tales, fables, myths, and even scriptures are passed down through the age-old tradition of storytelling. Stories have the power to engage our minds in a way that isolated facts, rules, or advice cannot. When we hear a story, we experience a world that is bigger than our own. We draw on our emotions to form a relationship with each character that we become attached to including the world in which they live. We like to imagine what we would do in their situation, or what life would be like in their world. We consider the complex problems they face, without feeling the fear and pressure of experiencing the issues ourselves. Imagine then what it does for a child's spirit and character to hear stories about Krishna's divine pastimes!

I encourage you to consider practicing the art of oral storytelling with your child. To prepare to tell a story, read through it yourself, read the example descriptions included in this book for each form, and look at a variety of artwork from that story. Retell the story in your own words, and not from memorizing. Make the story come to life with simple sound effects, and change the tone of your voice to reflect the emotions being felt in the story. After hearing a story a few times, your child may feel inspired to recreate small scenes from the story with you. Children love repetition, so be prepared to retell this story many times. These stories have many complex ideas for a child to learn from, and they can discover something new with each retelling. Each time you tell the same story, you will also gain confidence in your skill as a storyteller!

Each page in this book includes a recommendation of a devotional story to familiarize yourself with. If you do not have a copy of Srimad Bhagavatam or Krishna Book each story can be found through a quick online search. There are also short descriptions of each form being introduced or reviewed. Describe these forms as you tell the story so your child may paint a mental picture before you work on physically representing these forms in the following activities.

Walk the Forms

Lay down a long piece of string or rope in the shape of the form being introduced, and walk with your child barefoot along the path. This nurtures a child's need to move (as they cannot focus their mind with a restless body) while also encouraging a child's sense of balance and focus. Walking these forms may also create an emotional response from a child, which is a powerful way to ingrain something new in their mind.

Try this for yourself! Walk along each of these forms several times, and notice how your body reacts.

How does each make you feel? Personally, I feel that one invokes a feeling of peaceful wandering while the other requires a degree of precision and alertness.

When you walk a new form with your child, share these realizations and feelings with each other.

Sensory Play

Draw each form for your child on a chalkboard (or using chalk on a sidewalk outside) so they may trace it with their fingers. This provides a wonderful sensory experience. It is also a self correcting activity as the chalk will smudge showing the path their fingers take.

Hum or sing as you run your fingers along each form. How could the tone or pitch of your voice respond to the movement of your fingers? Perhaps on an upswing your voice reaches a higher pitch before lowering again as you draw your finger down. Maybe a form with sharp angles calls for a different tone than one with soft curves? Each person will interpret these forms in different ways, so explore the many possibilities by inviting others to join this activity.

Make a game to visually find new forms in everyday places and objects. Go on a form finding scavenger hunt, or collect items from around your home and take turns to describe each form you see.

Can you trace your fingers along the forms you find? These forms are not just random marks on paper a child has been told they must learn, but truly building blocks that makeup our world!

Drawing Forms

Using two pointer fingers and thumb, write new forms in the air using large full arm movements. Challenge your child to see what other body parts they can use to recreate each form! Can they trace it in the air with their nose? Or maybe their elbow? If a child struggles with this, you can stand opposite them and ask them to mirror your movements as you air draw the form.

Give your child a space to recreate these forms in the mud, sand, or a salt tray. This temporary form of writing provides a tactile experience and takes the pressure off of a child who may feel anxious about commiting a mark onto paper.

When your child is ready to write a new form on paper, there are several things you can do to set up good writing practices.

- ☐ Give your child blank paper to recreate each form, or use the tracing pages included in this book.
- ☐ Provide a variety of crayons so your child may choose the color they would like to use. Markers often feel easier for a child, but crayons are a better choice when learning to write. Crayons provide a more tactile experience, as a child can feel the texture of the paper as they mark the page. Crayons also require more muscle control in order to apply steady pressure.
- ☐ Find a comfortable surface where your child may sit, stand, or kneel with a nice posture. Their back, neck and arms should be unstrained and slouching should be discouraged.
- ☐ Encourage your child to draw these forms with full focus. It's better if your child sits for a few minutes and only writes one form with care, rather than fill up an entire page with rushed work. In time, creating these forms will be a mostly subconscious process, so avoid allowing the habit of careless writing to develop. If your child seems tired, agitated, or fidgety, it is best to revisit one of the activities that allow for full body movement or sensory play.
- ☐ To further exercise important arm and shoulder muscles for writing, you can ask your child to write vertically on a chalkboard or paper posted to the wall.

Get Creative

The forms presented in this book are purposefully simple. They are the foundational building blocks that makeup the shapes all around us. But with a little creativity a child can use these forms to create elaborate works of art.

- Challenge your child, and yourself with any of the following ideas:
- Design repeating patterns.
- Incorporate multiple bright colors.
- Apply transformations like: size, rotation, symmetry, or reflections across a line.
- Combine multiple forms to create a new design.
- Describe how you think the form might taste.
- Tell a new story that highlights a form.

There are examples of creative transformations throughout, but do not let these limit you. These are provided for inspiration only. Some of these ideas will be too advanced for your child while others may be uninspiring. Follow your child's lead and create something unique together!

Lessons

New Forms:

- ☐ Familiarize yourself with the story of Krishna Stealing the Butter
- ☐ Share the story with your child, paying special attention to the new forms being introduced:

  Krishna's body is adorned with strings of beautiful pearls, and rounded jewels.

  As Krishna tips the pot of butter, His delicious prize drips freely to the ground where He can share with the monkeys.

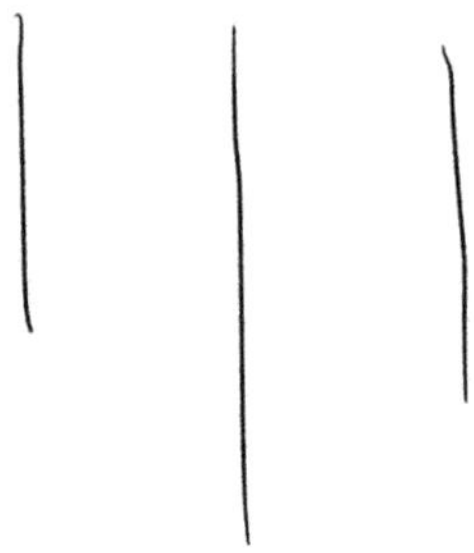

- ☐ Walk the Forms
- ☐ Sensory Play
- ☐ Draw the Forms
- ☐ Get Creative-

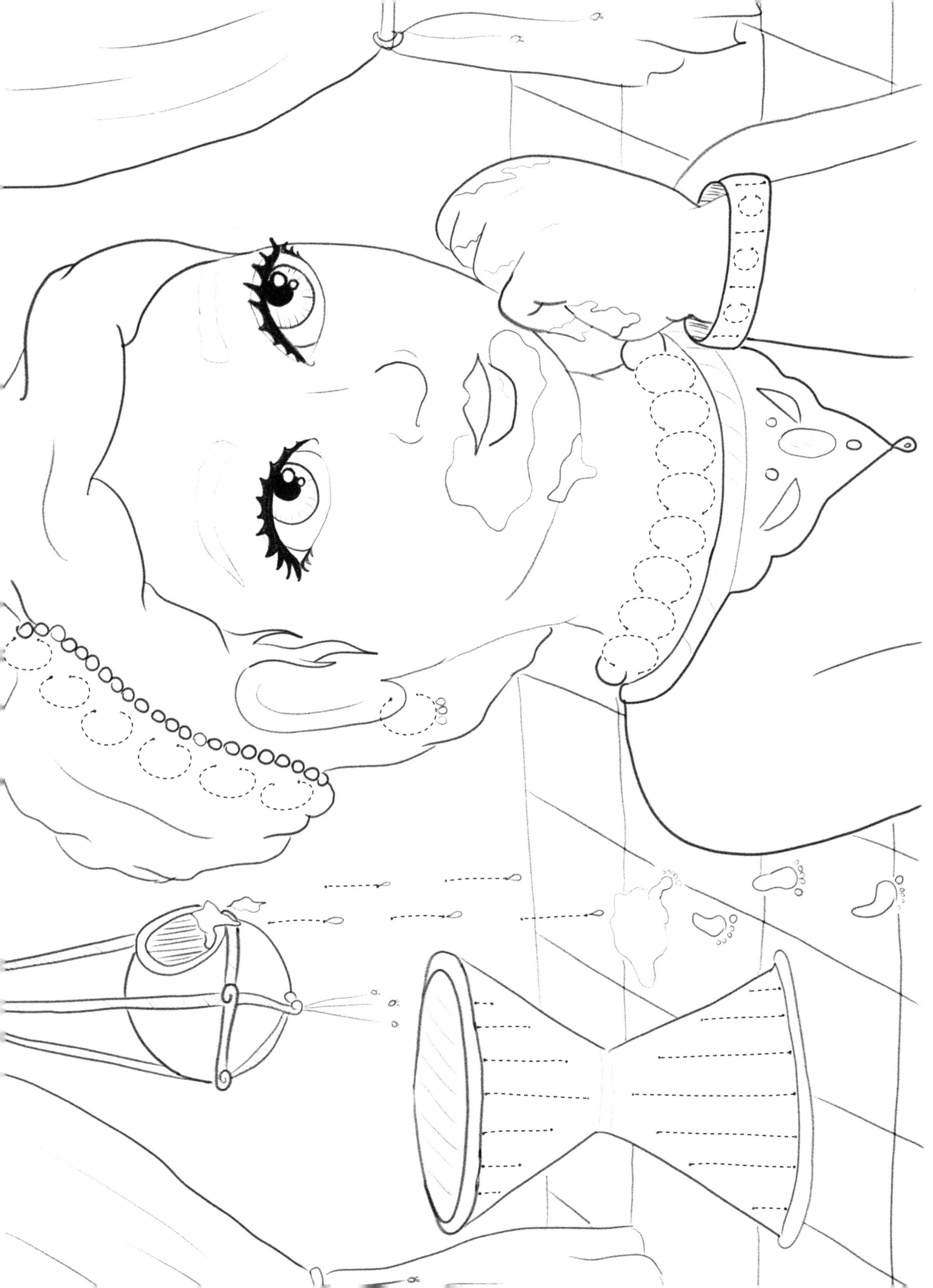

New Forms:

- ☐ Familiarize yourself with the story of Krishna Lifting Govardhan Hill
- ☐ Share the story with your child, paying special attention to the new forms being introduced:

Rain pours down from the storm clouds in many directions.

Water floods Govardhan Hill, causing streams to overflow and cascade to the ground like waterfalls.

- ☐ Walk the Forms
- ☐ Sensory Play- Go outside and create a hill from sand or dirt. Use your hands to dig curved stream forms into the side of your hill. Pour water to simulate rain and watch how the water flows and floods the streams.
- ☐ Draw the Forms
- ☐ Get Creative-

Familiar Forms:

Out of love for Krishna, the people of Vrindavan strive to serve Him by helping Him hold up the hill. They hold their sticks upright, and even though Krishna does not need their help, He lovingly accepts thier offering.

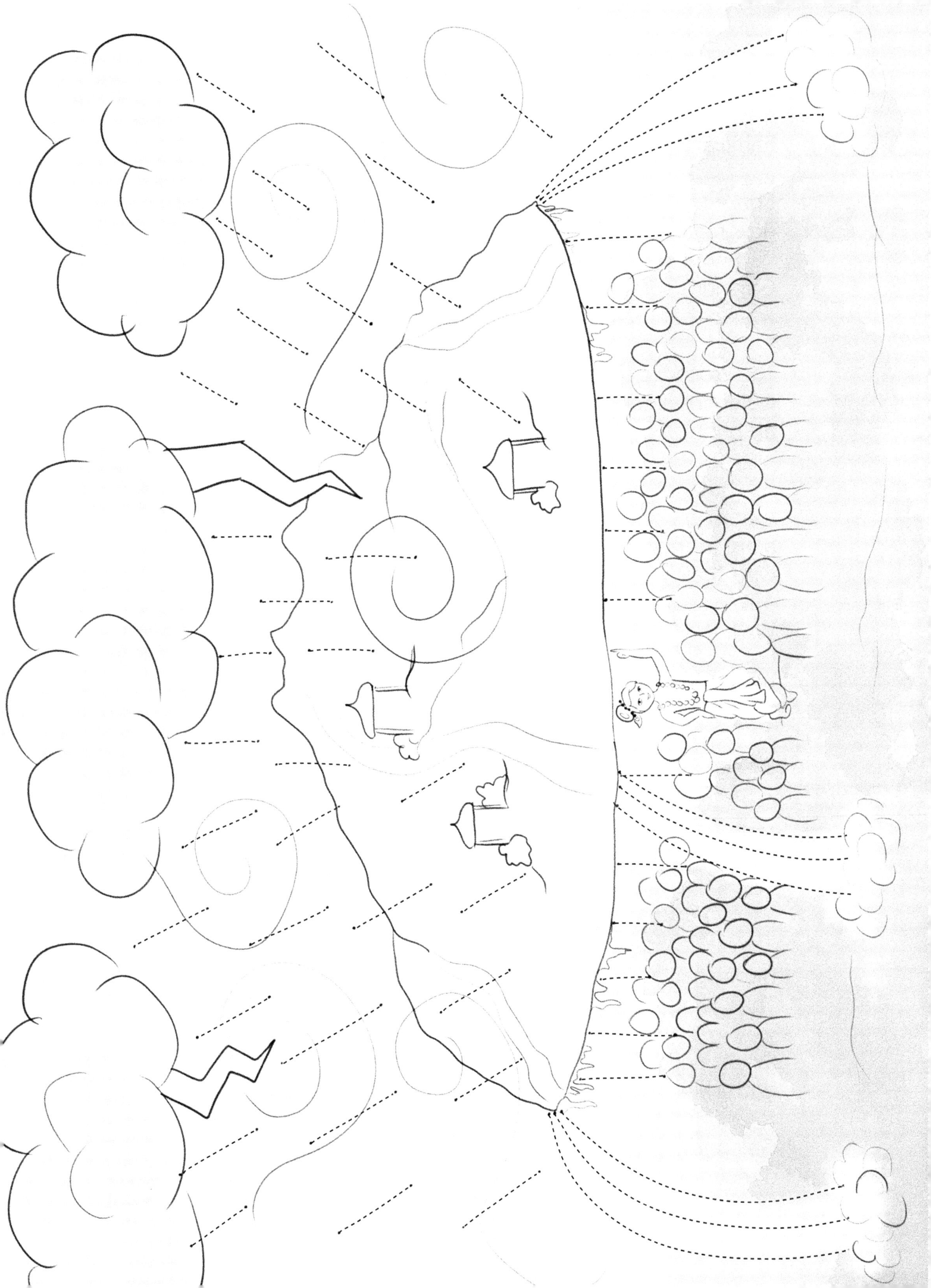

New Forms:

- ☐ Familiarize yourself with the story of Gajendra Moksha
- ☐ Share the story with your child, paying special attention to the new forms being introduced:

  Gajendra splashes and plays and creates waves that disturb the lake inhabitants.

  The crocodile sneaks up to strike Gajendra. Gajendra is too distracted to notice air bubbles coming closer.

  As the fight continues, it becomes apparent that every part of the crocodile is better suited for a life in the water. Even his large bony scales (scutes) with their jagged points protect his body from becoming weak.

- ☐ Walk the Forms
- ☐ Sensory Play
- ☐ Draw the Forms
- ☐ Get Creative- In this story, you can share how the water becomes turbulent as Gajendra plays, and then increases throughout thier battle.

Familiar Forms:

Birds soar high above the lake. Their wings catch the wind.

Sweet nectar fills the air, drawing butterflies to the garden.

Gajendra sprays water in all directions to cool his body.

New Forms:

- ☐ Familiarize yourself with gopi dots by searching for images online.
- ☐ Tell a story about a character decorating their (or a deity's) face with gopi dots for an upcoming festival. Pay special attention to the new forms being introduced:

I carefully swipe my brush along Krishna's cheek toward His nose. In one motion, I turn the brush as if to form a circle. I carefully turn my hand inward until His cheek is adorned with an elegant spiral.

- ☐ Walk the Forms
- ☐ Sensory Play- Paint your child's face using the new forms. Take turns describing the forms and how they feel. Challenge your child to guess which form you are drawing.
- ☐ Draw the Forms
- ☐ Get Creative- There is a blank gopi dots page in the back of this book so that your child may create their own designs.

Experiment with the size of spirals.

Familiar Forms:

I begin my design by painting small circles one after another above Krishna's eyebrows and down towards His cheeks.

Familiar Forms:

- ☐ Share with your child a story about a time when reading a great book transported your mind to a wonderful place!

- ☐ Using this illustration, brainstorm together what kind of story this child may be reading. Pay special attention to the forms that are being reviewed.

In the backyard:

The sun radiates its warmth in every direction. Sometimes, when the clouds part just right, the rays form long beams of light.

The fence is made from straight peices of wood. Each plank is cut with an angle on one end. When these are stood up together, a zig-zag runs along the top of the fence line.

In the Imagined World:

Butterflies and flowers may be small, but each has unique patterns and colors.

Lady bugs stand out in a garden because of their bright red body and black round spots.

Snail shells are quite unique with their beautiful spiraling form.

A bee twirls through the air to greet Radharani.

Familiar Forms:

- ☐ Familiarize yourself with the traditional pottery art from India by searching for online images.

- ☐ Using this illustration, encourage your child to describe each form using some of the following prompts:

  What do you think this pot was used for?

  Who do you think painted these beautiful designs?

  What does this form remind you of?

  What do you like about this design?

  What do you think other side of this pot looks like?

  Forms being reviewed:

- ☐ Get Creative- Clay pot painting is a fun way for children to enjoy sensory play as well as practice their own form drawing. Even simple modeling clay will work!   There is a blank clay pot included in the back of this book that a child may use to create their own designs.

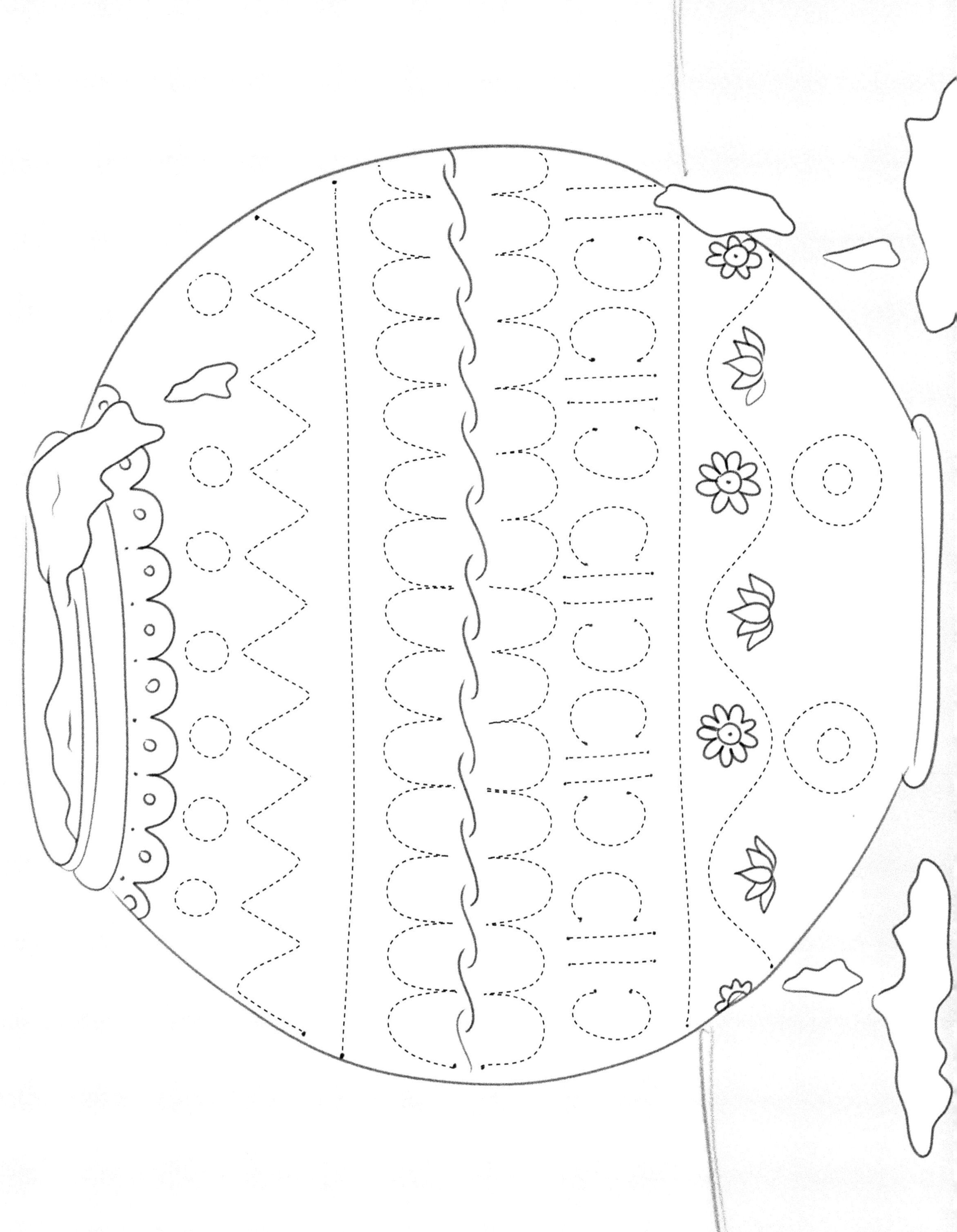

Mazes encourage a child to hold a writing utensil with care and to think about where they want to draw their lines.

The mazes in this book have many possible solutions so that a new writer can find success without becoming frustrated by too challenging a puzzle.

New Forms:

- [ ] Familiarize yourself with the story of Krishna defeating Trinavarta.

- [ ] Share the story with your child, paying special attention to the new forms being introduced:

The whirlwind demon takes hold of Krishna. The wind whips back and forth starting wide at the top, and gradually narrowing down to a single point, forming a great tornado.

- [ ] Walk the Forms- Pretend to be a spinning tornado! Stand tall, with arms open wide to form the funnel, then whirl around while acting out this pastime.

- [ ] Sensory Play

- [ ] Draw the Forms

- [ ] Get Creative

Familiar Forms:

From the top of each tornado, you can see the winds spiraling downward to the ground.

Trinavarta is so fierce that even the large jagged mountains tremble from the force of the wind.

New Forms:

- [ ] Familiarize yourself with the story of Krishna and the Kaliya serpent.
- [ ] Share the story with your child, paying special attention to the new forms being introduced:

Kaliya thrashes and writhes. He disturbs the water and creates huge waves. The waves chase each other towards the shore.

- [ ] Walk the Forms
- [ ] Sensory Play
- [ ] Draw the Forms
- [ ] Get Creative

Familiar Forms:

Each of Kaliya's many heads can be seen curving above the water.

New Forms:

- ☐ Familiarize yourself with the descriptions of how Krishna plays a flute.
- ☐ Share the story with your child, paying special attention to the new forms being introduced:

Even the bees dance in the air at the sound of Krishna's flute. Mesmerized by this trancendental sound, the bees fly towards Krishna while dancing in circles all the way.

- ☐ Walk the Forms
- ☐ Sensory Play
- ☐ Draw the Forms
- ☐ Get Creative-

Two bees dance together!

Experiment with how each bee could dance.

Familiar Forms:

Krishna's thick long hair is placed atop His head by twirling it round and round into a spiral forming a bun.

This bun is adorened by a string of round pearls.

New Forms:

- ☐ Familiarize yourself with the story of Domodara Lila.
- ☐ Share the story with your child, paying special attention to the new forms being introduced:

The rope twists around Krishna's waist, keeping Him tied in place. Each strand is wrapped in turn over the next to form a long rope.

In the mood of a scolded child, Krishna's face becomes covered in large tears dripping from His eyes.

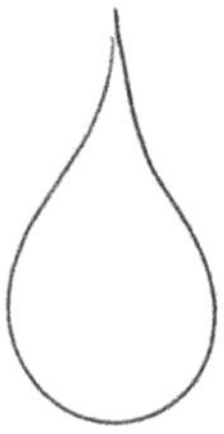

- ☐ Walk the Forms
- ☐ Sensory Play- Look for a large twisted rope, chunky yarn, or twist lengths of fabric together. Let your child touch and feel the forms that are created. How far can you follow one twisting line along the rope?
- ☐ Draw the Forms
- ☐ Get Creative

Familiar Forms:

Mother Yashoda wraps the ropes round and round to form strong knots that will keep Krishna from causing more mischief.

Even as an angry child, Krishna's beauty radiates like a light from His body.

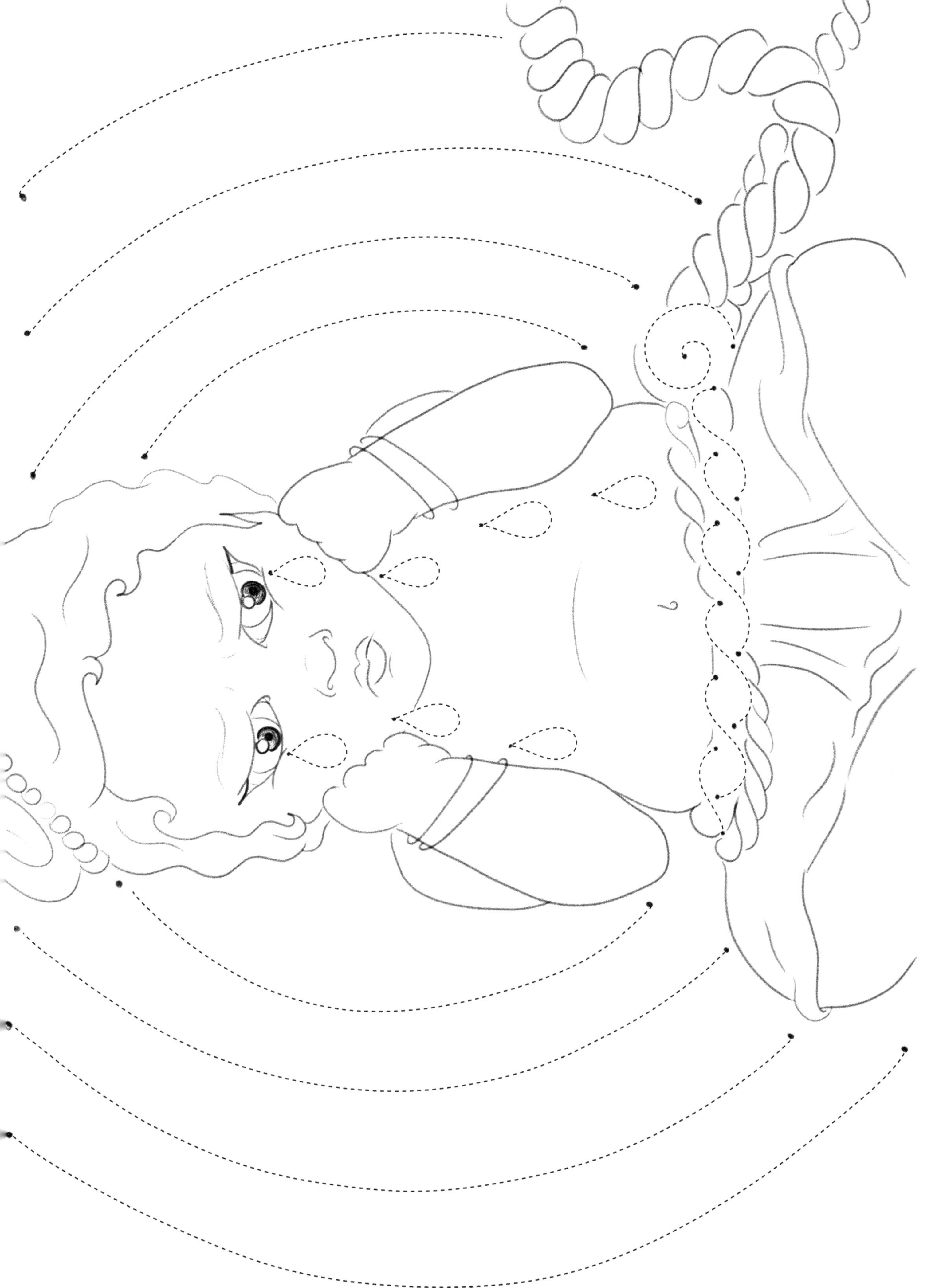

New Forms:

- ☐ Familiarize yourself with gopi dots by searching for images online.
- ☐ Tell a story about a character decorating their (or a deity's) face with gopi dots for an upcoming festival. Pay special attention to the new forms being introduced:

With my brush, I draw a small hump
just above the start of Krishna's eyebrow.
Without lifting my brush, I make another
hump next to it, this time taller, then one
more again, but this time shorter.

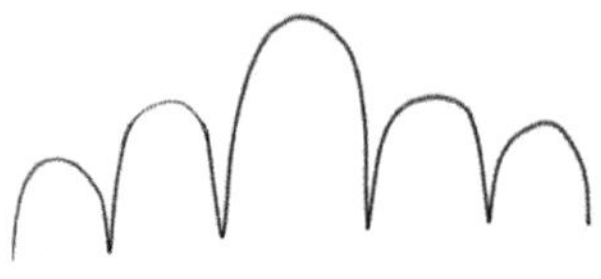

- ☐ Walk the Forms
- ☐ Sensory Play- Paint your child's face using the new forms. Take turns describing the forms and how they feel. Challenge your child to guess which form you are drawing.
- ☐ Draw the Forms
- ☐ Get Creative- There is a blank gopi dots page in the back of this book so that your child may create their own designs.

Familiar Forms:

Throughout the design, I like to
form little colored dots.

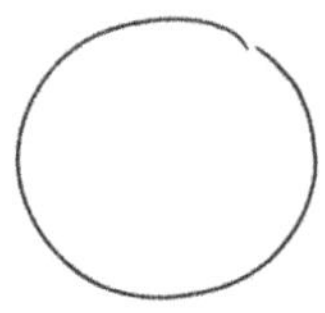

Vines swoop around each
flower in a graceful curve. Some
are long, but around each bud, I
draw them very small.

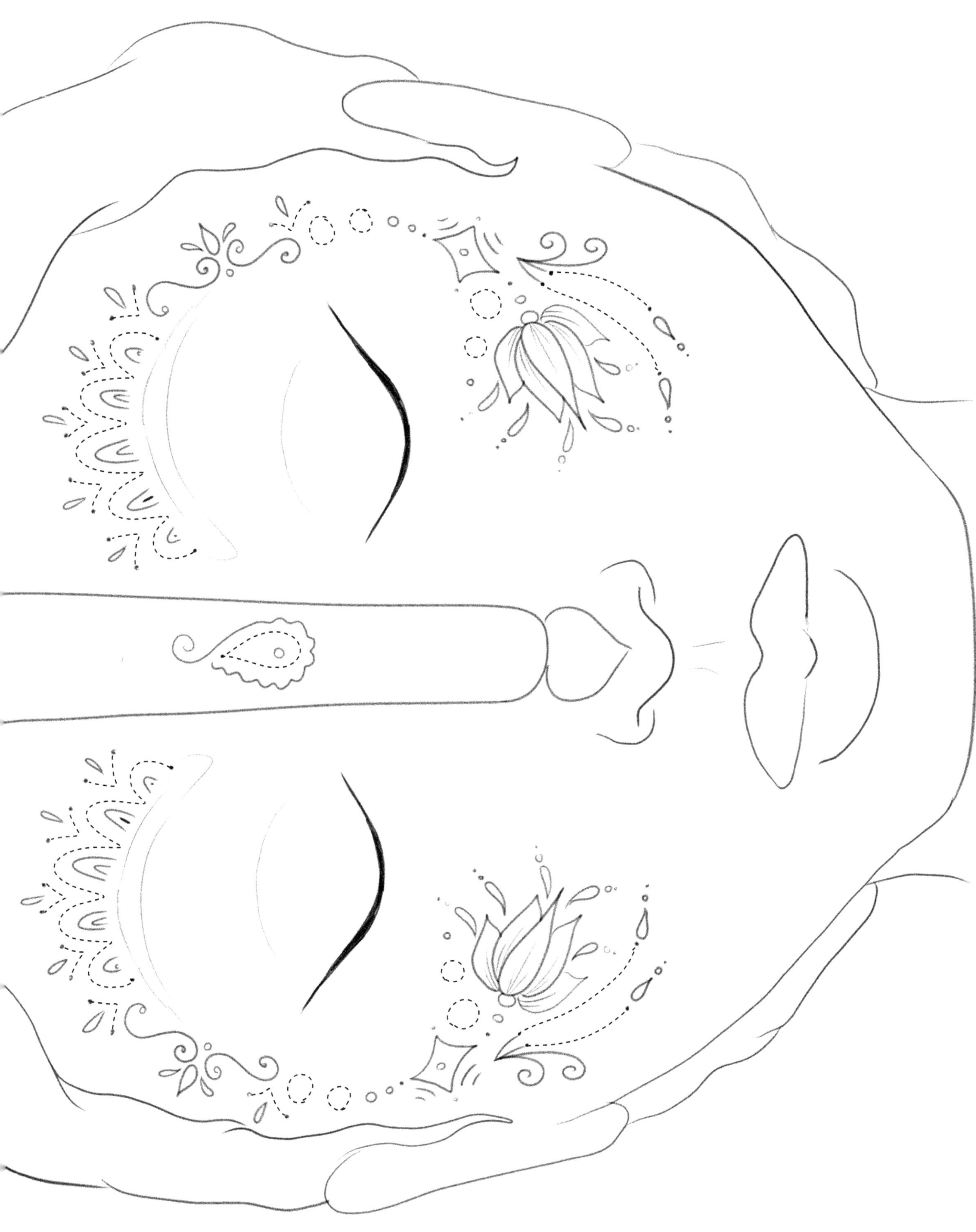

Familiar Forms:

- [ ] Familiarize yourself with the traditional pottery art from India by searching for online images.

- [ ] Using this illustration, encourage your child to describe each form using some of the following prompts:

  What do you think this pot was used for?

  Who do you think painted these beautiful designs?

  What does this form remind you of?

  What do you like about this design?

  What do you think other side of this pot looks like?

Forms being reviewed:

- [ ] Get Creative- Clay pot painting is a fun way for children to enjoy sensory play as well as practice their own form drawing. Even simple modeling clay will work! There is a blank clay pot included in the back of this book that a child may use to create their own designs.

Mazes encourage a child to hold a writing utensil with care and to think about where they want to draw their lines.

The mazes in this book have many possible solutions so that a new writer can find success without becoming frustrated by too challenging a puzzle.

New Forms:

- ☐ The lotus flower is used as a symbol in many Srimad Bhagavatam stories. Each may highlight a different quality of this bloom, so there is not just one story or quality I suggest for this form. Instead, choose whichever story you like. Another option is to describe the lotus flower's qualities like shape, habitat, color, and aroma. Next time your child hears a story that highlights the lotus flower, they will be able to create a full image in their mind.

- ☐ Share your story with your child, paying special attention to the new forms being introduced:

Each lotus bud is tightly packed with flower petals waiting to expand. This packet of petals has a wide base where many small petals grow. The largest petals fold together like praying hands.

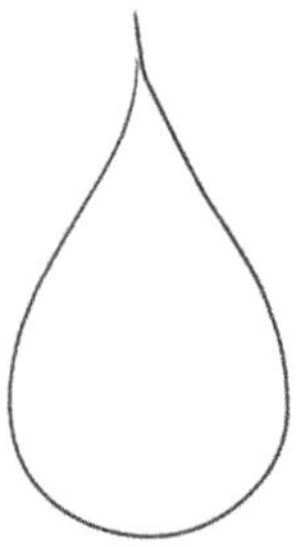

As each petal grows larger, the flower opens and invites small beetles to drink its nectar.

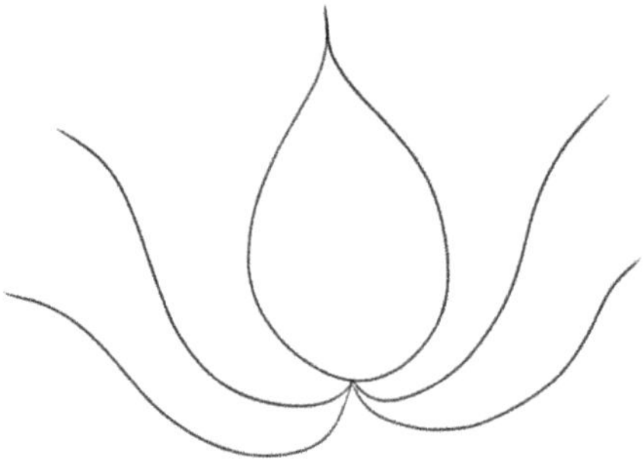

- ☐ Walk the Forms

- ☐ Sensory Play

- ☐ Draw the Forms

- ☐ Get Creative- Can you draw lotuses opening wider and wider?

Familiar Forms:

The seed pod of the lotus, has a wide round top which holds many smaller round seeds.

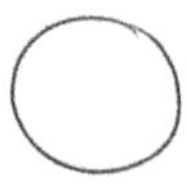

Along the edge of the water, you will often find tall grass which bends slightly to shade the water.

New Forms:

- [ ] Familiarize yourself with the tradition of offering obeisances.

- [ ] Tell your child a story about a time when you or a imaginary character offered obeisances to a Krishna deity, paying special attention to the new forms being introduced:

When I offer obeisances, my head touches the ground and my spine gradually slopes upwards where it meets my legs in a smooth curve. My legs fold towards my body where my bent knees create a sharp angle so that my feet extend behind me.

- [ ] Walk the Forms

- [ ] Sensory Play- How many forms can you see in the carved alter?

- [ ] Draw the Forms

- [ ] Get Creative- Use previous forms to decorate the pillars.

New Forms:

- ☐ Familiarize yourself with the story of Krishna stealing the gopi's clothes.
- ☐ Share the story with your child, paying special attention to the new forms being introduced:

Krishna is surrounded by so many beautiful garments. Each has a different design sewn into the trim. The threads swirl and loop down the entire length of the colorful saris.

- ☐ Walk the Forms
- ☐ Sensory Play- Look through trims and fabric that have embroidered designs. (If you do not have many fancy clothes, walk around a fabric store.) Run your fingers along the designs and look for familiar forms.
- ☐ Draw the Forms
- ☐ Get Creative

New Forms:

- [ ] Familiarize yourself with the story of Krishna defeating Aghasura.
- [ ] Share the story with your child, paying special attention to the new forms being introduced:

The cowherd boys use Agha's body like a playground. They climb his large scaly side, then slide down his smooth body towards the ground

- [ ] Walk the Forms
- [ ] Sensory Play
- [ ] Draw the Forms
- [ ] Get Creative-

Make all sorts of slides! Tall slides, windy slides, what can you dream up?

New Forms:

- [ ] Familiarize yourself with the story of Krishna swallowing up the forest fire.

- [ ] Share the story with your child, paying special attention to the new forms being introduced:

The trees of the forest reach high into the sky like arrows standing on end. For as far as you can see, these giants are packed close together forming a continuous canopy across the horizon.

- [ ] Walk the Forms

- [ ] Sensory Play

- [ ] Draw the Forms

- [ ] Get Creative- Use pictures of various tree types growing in your region challenge your child to try creating a forest canopy or tree line using those general shapes.

Familiar Forms:

- ☐ Familiarize yourself with the traditional pottery art from India by searching for online images.

- ☐ Using this illustration, encourage your child to describe each form using some of the following prompts:

  What do you think this pot was used for?

  Who do you think painted these beautiful designs?

  What does this form remind you of?

  What do you like about this design?

  What do you think other side of this pot looks like?

Forms being reviewed:

- ☐ Get Creative- Clay pot painting is a fun way for children to enjoy sensory play as well as practice their own form drawing. Even simple modeling clay will work! There is a blank clay pot included in the back of this book that a child may use to create their own designs.

Mazes encourage a child to hold a writing utensil with care and to think about where they want to draw their lines.

The mazes in this book have many possible solutions so that a new writer can find success without becoming frustrated by too challenging a puzzle.

Use the following pages to create your own unique designs!

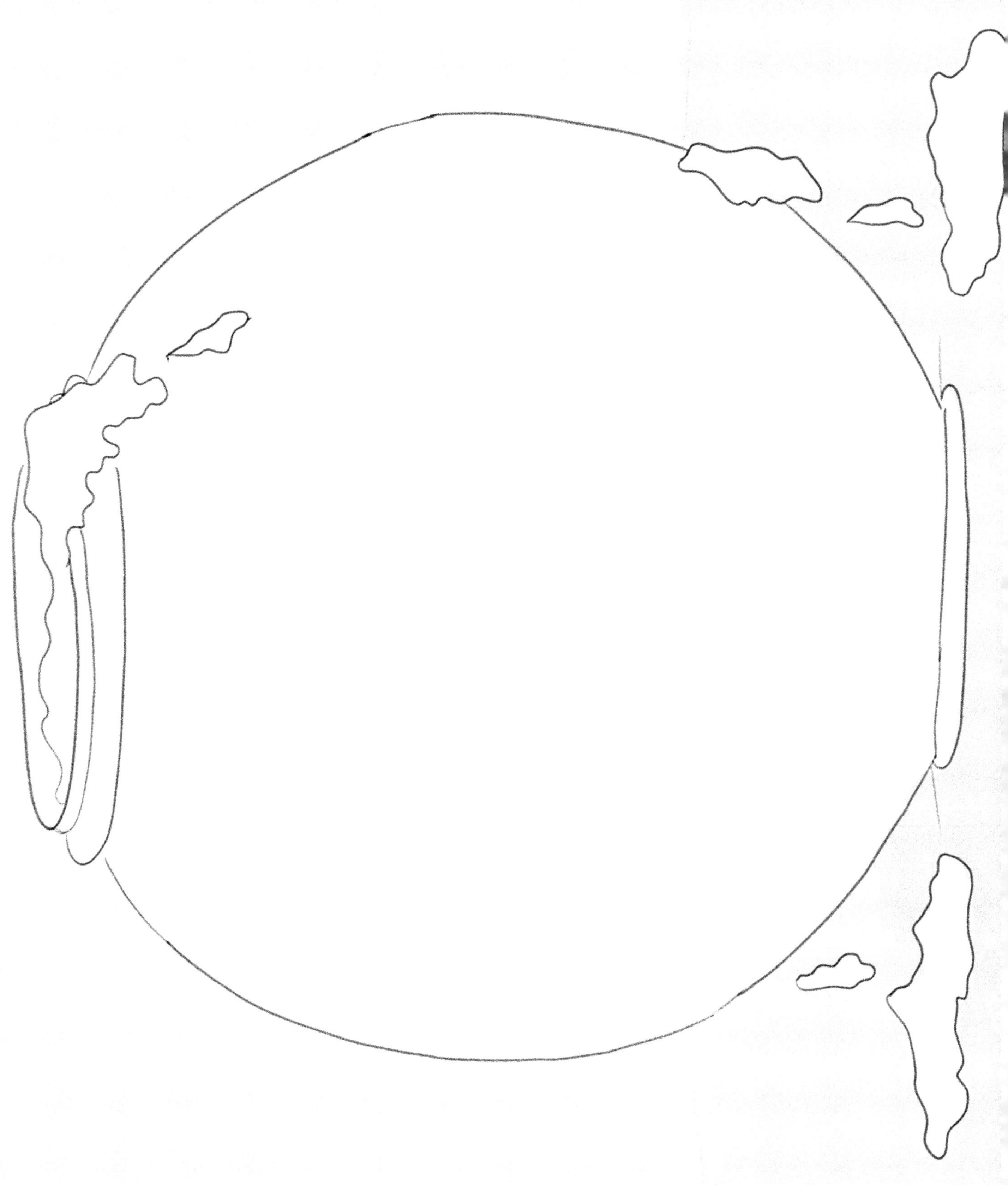

www.ingramcontent.com/pod-product-compliance
Ingram Content Group UK Ltd.
Pitfield, Milton Keynes, MK11 3LW, UK
UKHW051135260726
13967UKWH00010B/3061